Safe Hands, Safe Hair

A Narrative Therapy book for Young Children with Trichotillomania

Written by Dr. Anna Dacus and Illustrated by Jeremy Wells

First Printing edition 2020 in United States

AD Publishing
P.O. Box 152
Lyons, IL 60534

DEDICATED TO MY AMAZING FAMILY!

My name is Dr. Anna Dacus, and I am a licensed clinical psychologist who has spent my entire career working with children and adolescents. I am also a mother, and when my daughter turned 15 months old, she began pulling out her hair. This was beyond challenging as a parent, and I shed many tears that symbolized my feelings of helplessness. Every child's journey will be different, although I am happy to say that my daughter has outgrown her hair pulling behavior and has learned to engage in healthy coping alternatives. This was not an easy journey, but I found that consistency, patience, redirection, blocking the behavior and positive reinforcement were key! I wrote this book because when looking and needing, I found that there were many books out there for me to read as a parent about my daughter's behavior. However, I was not able to find any books for me as a parent to read to my daughter.

As parents, one of the tools that we have to help our children understand and process various challenges throughout their development is narrative therapy: aka story time. By reading our children social stories, they are able to gain an increased awareness of themselves as an individual as well as themselves in relation to others. This process allows children to advance in their development by learning how to identify the various feelings that they experience along with healthy ways to cope and manage those feelings. Children who have trichotillomania often utilize hair pulling as a coping/self-soothing strategy to manage various feelings such as worry, boredom, and/or frustration. I hope that you find this book useful in helping you to work with your child to normalize his/her feelings as well as to gain alternative adaptive coping skills to replace the hair pulling behavior.

My body has two feet, wiggle wiggle.

My body has two hands, clap clap.

My body has one head,

Mom sometimes calls it my thinking cap.

Sometimes, when I get bored, my hands start to pull my hair.

But then, I remember that I have to take safe care.

To help my hair stay safe, I wear a headband.

It looks super stylish with my long, curly strands.

Hair is not for pulling, it stays on my head.

So, what are safe things

that I can do with my hands instead?

Well, hands are for high fives and playing in sand.

Hands are for squishing play dough
and banging on pans.

Hands are for putting on lotion
that makes them feel smooth.

Hands are for helping me eat salty, sour, sweet, and sometimes spicy foods.

Sometimes, when I feel worried, my hands start to fidget

So I make a safe choice, and I find my gadget.

Sometimes, when I am sleepy, my hands want to pull my hair.

So I wear my Scratch Sleeves sleep shirt,

and Mom shows me that she cares.

Mom said if I make safe hair choices, I can earn a pom-pom.
So I work hard to do safe things that help me feel calm.

And, when I earn enough pom-poms to fill up my jar,
I get to pick a treat because I've worked so very hard.

very day, I will try my best to make safe hand and hair choices.

And as I grow, I will strengthen my voice.

ecause my feelings are important, no matter what they are,

and sometimes talking about them may prove to be hard.

But, I will practice and learn and do my very best!
With the help of my grown-up, I will master
this safe hair conquest!

www.ingramcontent.com/pod-product-compliance
Lightning Source LLC
Chambersburg PA
CBHW080927050426
42334CB00055B/2838